For Real

Ben Wilkinson

smith|doorstop

Published 2014 by
smith|doorstop Books
The Poetry Business
Bank Street Arts
32–40 Bank Street
Sheffield S1 2DS

ISBN 978-1-910367-07-0
Typeset by Utter
Printed by People for Print, Sheffield

Acknowledgements
Thanks to the editors of the following publications, where most of these poems first appeared: *Edinburgh Review*, *The Guardian*, *Liverpool FC Monthly*, *Poetry London*, *Poetry Review*, *The Spectator*, *The Times Literary Supplement*.
'The Catch' was inspired by a visual artwork by Tom de Freston.
An earlier version of 'Lights out' was published in *The Sparks* (tall-lighthouse, 2008). 'This is Anfield' is for Lynn, Paul and Sam.

smith|doorstop Books are a member of Inpress:
www.inpressbooks.co.uk. Distributed by Central Books Ltd.,
99 Wallis Road, London E9 5LN

The Poetry Business is an Arts Council
National Portfolio Organisation

Contents

This pamphlet is dedicated to Helen, with love and admiration.

That's shit. I'm not putting it right. I can't make you feel what I felt.

– David Foster Wallace,
Brief Interviews with Hideous Men

Why love if losing hurts so much? I have no answers anymore, only the life I have lived. Twice in that life I've been given the choice: as a boy, and as a man. The boy chose safety, the man chooses suffering. The pain now is part of the happiness then. That's the deal.

– C. S. Lewis, as portrayed
by Anthony Hopkins in *Shadowlands*

The Catch

For you, the catch wasn't something caught:
not word or contender, attention or fire.
Not the almost-missed train, or the sort
of wave surfers might wait an entire
lifetime for. Not the promise that leaves
the old man adrift for days, his boat
creaking, miles offshore. Nor what cleaves
the heart in two, that left your throat
parched and mute for taking pill
after yellow-green pill, the black-blue
taste the price you paid to kill
the two-parts sadness to one-part anger.
No. The catch was what you could never
let go. It's what you carried, and still do.

The Nightmare

Remember that long drive back from the Lakes,
lightning-lit through endless rain?
Nights I dream us on that stretch again,
the road a river with a line of silver
that leaps about its centre;
leading us to Newby, Lawkland, Cleatop.

These times, though, the car shudders
like someone about to vomit –
a thunderbolt, throwing
us forward through time
with the dashboard dials spinning;
making a DeLorean out of your Yaris.

The windscreen warps with scenery,
a zoetrope at full tilt.
We watch the road narrow
into a dirt track, cars evaporate,
trees shrivel into nothing
while others burst up in their place.

Dumbstruck, we sit in its wake.
And I want to tell you the world
we find is a glorious one,
paradise pooled in light,
but I can't. Stepping
into heat, a murder of crows

scatters in the field to the west;
the trees diagrams of harm,
the earth barren in a stony calm.
Walking, silence for what seems
like hours. Then, when I turn to say
as much, you're nowhere to be found.

The nightmare should end there.
Instead I carry on, hopelessly
trekking a dust trail. All to find
nothing apart from that outline
in the heat, a shape
on the horizon. It's then I wake.

Above Stanage

When else but that day we were caught on the ridge
in a storm so fierce in its sudden grip
fields moved like water?

And how the wind
tore a path there before us;
the landscape loosened from its guy ropes.

Farcical, like something out of a Brontë novel,
with that touch of the realistic absurd –
our umbrella flung inside out

and you hardly uttering a word ...
Here again, I struggle to turn it back on itself.
As if I'm not soaked already. As if we might work things out.

The River Don

rushes by, a current pushing on
past rows of fig trees blooming from its banks
and factory outfalls, spilling nearby.
Remember how the floods two years back
rose to the mark on The Fat Cat's wall –
that third summer of ours when the rain did
nothing but pour, the thought of what we might
wake to that dream of mine, the same dream
on/off for weeks?

It never reached us. We didn't
climb downstairs half-asleep to find our furniture
floating, or ornaments, CDs and kept cassette tapes
making their bids to escape. Instead, the house
sat safe and sound – floors dry, photo frames still,
something else edging closer, the way water will.

Stag

The one I saw on the bypass that night –
antlers like a winter oak
as it strode from the roadside –
came again in a dream; keeping
its distance as it does every time.

When I met it for real I kept mine:
a stalled presence
on a stretch without streetlights;
its silhouette held there
before it turned and left.

In the dream, though, I follow –
into fields and meadows
where it spots me, begins to trot,
picks up pace before bolting off.
What if I could get close enough,

look it in those cavernous eyes?
What else could I hope to find
but yours, as all you said
echoes in my mind,
its glare passing through me?

First Glance

Like *that*, the hell-bent flap
of a pigeon at the window –
as if startled, livid

at my lifting some slim volume
from a shelf,
rather than trapped,

taking glass for air
and flailing against a trick
of the light –

reminds me of that time I saw
what I thought was you
(before I truly knew you)

kissing someone else,
only to find you later, strolling
up the road I was traipsing down.

Lights out

Halfway through plates of biryani
and the National Grid plunges us
into darkness. I haven't a clue

where the torch is, forget candles,
and it strikes me all we can do
is wait this out; break bread

and top up our glasses
as moonlight spills
into the garden. This absence

of illumination, the TV's hum,
seems inhuman, sends us
back to something further –

sketched outlines of faces,
the pulse of our hearts –
how we once saw the nights

as animals ...
now my flicking the Zippo open
and setting down its flame

lights up our eyes,
these familiar surroundings,
as if the first

scratch-spark of wood or flint;
the filmic flash and blink
as sixty-watts brings us back to life.

Hound

When it comes, and I know how it comes
from nowhere, out of night
like a shadow falling on streets,
how it waits by the door in silence –
a single black thought, its empty face –

don't let it tie you down to the house,
don't let it slope upstairs to spend
hours coiled next to your bed,
but force the thing out, make it trudge
for miles in cold and wind and sleet.

Have it follow you, the faithful pet
it pretends to be, this mutt
like a poor-man's Cerberus,
tell it where to get off when it hangs
on with its coaxing look,

leave it tethered to a lamppost
and forget those pangs of guilt.
Know it's no dog but a phantom,
fur so dark it gives back nothing,
see your hand pass through

its come-and-go presence,
air of self-satisfied deception,
just as the future bursts in on
the present, its big *I am*, and that
sulking hound goes to ground again.

The Leash

Snow ploughed up high on the pavements
and snow still drifting down,
us, wandering back from Rivelin at dusk
tired, slipping in bad shoes
and wrapped in long winter coats,

remember bumping into that drunk
and his flea-bitten dog?
I felt for that Staffie, bloodshot eyes
and bark worse than its bite,
even as it sniffed out my fear

to start snapping at my side.
We laughed about it afterwards –
me skittering on ice as it leapt around –
but I swear its look of anger was
sadness, leashed tight to the here and now.

This is Anfield

Living up to its fabled buzz, the Kop roared and rose
even before kick-off. Down in the main stand
I watched; John Barnes adjusting his captain's band
on the hallowed turf. Waves of red in rows
and rows – a kid in that season's kit, I swelled
with a kind of borrowed pride, belonging
without belonging; my dad and brother craning
to see McManaman darting, how Fowler propelled
strike after strike.

                                        Half-time over, and a crashing header
left the keeper without a chance ... the place erupted.
I still remember it like that – the luminous pitch,
the echo of the terraces, players floodlit
beneath an October sky. An ordinary game,
solid win, save for one kid looking on in wonder.

Bearing

Watching him that spring-spilled-into-summer,
sat among Algar Seco's jagged rocks,

steadfast with rod, tub of bait,
water, hunk of bread,

still as a stork in its nest
settled above the walls of Silves,

I recovered what it was to wait –
content, not out of hope or faith

but for the catch that always comes;
a clutch of silver by dusk

like us, stumbling onto the beach one night,
finding that added depth in each other's eyes.

Rooms

That amber light colouring the walls
  as we took the stairs up one by one,
leaving the last sparks of the fire
  to sink into embers and dark.

If I'd turned back then, I could think on
  that room's evidence: pore over
a guitar's silent moan, fag butts
  and empties – its version of events.

As if it might lend the clues that,
   pieced into some sort of sense,
would make our later rush
  seem selfish, or strangely selfless.

Let's say it was both. Funny how you
  can find yourself lost in the world,
lost in another's arms, like finding out
  all you thought you knew was wrong.

There are mornings I wake
  not to alarms or the radio's talk,
but with the dream of that room
  which, for a moment, still rings truest.

Camouflage

Like the chameleon that changes
colour to fight
or attract the attention of a mate

(not, as the myth runs,
to match its background
in nothing more than coincidence)

I came to realise my big mistake
was arguing for the sake of it –
left at the Lescar's bar

with fists propping my cheeks,
or those nights spent alone
on our sofa, dreary as the surroundings.

October

after Paul Verlaine

Here it comes now – autumn's evening –
the setting sun sparking leaves into life.
Death fills the fields with its single word
like the *thwack* of a kitchen knife.

Nothing comes close to the truest season,
free of summer's callow passions.
Watch it wait with its store of darkness,
making sketches of all that might happen.

Of course those nutters and pushovers
all go for spring and dawn, lovers who
looked better the drunken night before.

Me? I'll take autumn's cruel stare
over summer's pining dove.
Its cold, sharp glance is the real look of love.

The Argument

still stews in the hearts of these two –
a flaw in the foundations of the tall terraced house
they moved to six months back: this lass who, just now,
is sat upstairs on a bed, coaxing notes from a clarinet

as her guy props the tent of Frost's *A Witness Tree*
on the breakfast bar, looks at the yard, flicks the kettle on.
A cold winter: their first under the same roof. The sun
skim-reads them through separate windows.

And it isn't that they won't come through this, but what
the house alone, insidious, is able to articulate. Half-empty
cups on a table. A dust-thick windowsill. A washer spinning
through its final cycle, like a HGV thundering downhill.

The Balcony

after Eugenio Montale

Remember those nights I'd wait below
as you stood in the stars? We'd talk
of leaving, me auditioning for Romeo,
fluffing my lines as usual.

Now on the other side I lean smoking,
think on that handful of chances.
The latticework of a tower block
a chessboard cleared after stalemate.

Somewhere your side of the Atlantic
you cup your hands, light one up. Here
it starts raining as I hang in the moment,
turn to this window's squaring of dark.

The Beach

Again, the dream comes: I find myself
on this windswept stretch at dawn.

The surf's spray hits the rocks.
A half-moon hangs in drifting fog.

And all at once, the tang of that sweet,
salt-sharp breeze on my tongue.

Strips of light cut through the dark.
This dream-in-a-dream that always leads

to your house, our private little coast ...
the contoured sands of the sheets,

our shadows blurred on the walls.
Then the taste of your cunt

as you come, and the whole scene
shakes and stalls.

What I'd give to find that beach for real.
Back to you, and all we had before.

The Door

What was it that brought us out that day
from pints and talk, our corner snug,
down streets still slick with rain?

A mist had thickened to clinging fog –
the road deserted except distant traffic,
blinking away like lifeboats at sea.

Forgetting ourselves, it seemed a trick
when the city gave way to fields, empty
as all we weren't saying, but thinking.

I'm thinking now of that barn we saw.
Dilapidated, abandoned; sparrows darting
from its roof; but most of all the door

where no door was, bricked up
yet suddenly revealing itself,
like a portal between worlds.

Let's say it was. Let's say all we felt
stood there, all we've held off. Let's walk
through that door, love, and never look back.